D0911025

Gratitude:

How to Appreciate Life's Gifts

Edited by Kathryn Britton and Senia Maymin

POSITIVE PSYCHOLOGY NEWS SERIES

Gratitude:

How to Appreciate Life's Gifts

Series Editor: Senia Maymin
Book Editor: Kathryn Britton

Positive Psychology News, LLC

2010

www.PositivePsychologyNews.com
Positive Psychology News Daily

ISBN: 145387867X

EAN-13: 9781453878675

Cover art by Edward Glen Britton

Internal illustrations by Kevin Gillespie

Printed in the United States of America

The second book of the Positive Psychology News series is dedicated with gratitude to

All the authors and people who have posted comments at Positive Psychology News Daily. They have made the site a vibrant and growing community.

Books in the Positive Psychology News Series

Resilience: How to Navigate Life's Curves

Gratitude: How to Appreciate Life's Gifts

See http://PositivePsychologyNews.com for links to order.

A STORY

If you fall while hiking in the woods and get an 8-inch bruise, you could have several responses. One could be "Wow, thank goodness I didn't break my leg because it sure would have been hard for my husband to carry me back to the car." This reaction would be a type of gratitude, gratitude for an event that didn't happen.

I learned of this type of thinking from an article written by Kathryn Britton on Positive Psychology News Daily. How often have we had events like this? The heart-pounding relief and adrenaline of a near car collision. Or the happiness that a friend did not lose a job? Or having a health issue resolved? We can all imagine the darker things that didn't happen.

Psychologists call this counter-factual thinking, being aware of what could have happened as well as the facts of the actual event that did happen. Recent research from Berkeley has shown that people who engage in positive counterfactual thinking, such as "Well at least that didn't happen" tend to be happier than ones who do not. In particular, people who imagine not having met their spouses report many more feelings of warmth and happiness toward their spouses.

According to psychologist, Robert Emmons, "The grateful person senses that much goodness happens quite independently of his actions or even in spite of himself." Awareness of this goodness, including awareness of mischance avoided, is a major ingredient of well-being.

WHO YOU ARE

You may be a student of psychology. Or you may want to appreciate life more. Or you may be a coach and want to pick up tips and tools to share with your clients.

WHO WE ARE

We are authors at *Positive Psychology News Daily* (http://PositivePsychologyNews.com).

Perhaps you wonder what positive psychology is. In 1998 as president of the American Psychological Association, Dr. Martin Seligman issued a call to action that changed the direction of psychology. He asked his colleagues to be just as interested in building the best things in life as in repairing the worst.

Since then, Seligman has gone on to found the Master of Applied Positive Psychology (MAPP) program at the University of Pennsylvania (Penn) in 2005. Students in the program are established professionals in law, medicine, education, and business. In 2010, around 200 students from around the world have graduated from the Penn program. Similar MAPP programs have started in the United Kingdom, Israel, Mexico, Australia, and Italy. The mission of these programs is to equip people to use research findings to make a positive difference in the world.

The articles in this book are drawn from the growing collection of articles published online in Positive Psychology News Daily. Most of the authors are graduates of MAPP programs. In late 2010, Positive Psychology News Daily has over 60 authors, over 800 articles, over 6,000 discussion comments, and over 1 million visits. Recently, associate editor Kathryn Britton and I started talking about bringing these articles to a broader audience. It's compelling research. It works.

A year ago, Kathryn and I created the first little book in the *Positive Psychology News* series on resilience, incorporating many of the superb research-based articles on the site combined with insightful comments from readers.

This little book on gratitude is Kathryn's brainchild. Kathryn has been interested in the role of gratitude in human well-being for as long as we have been working together. She suggested this as the next topic for the Positive Psychology News book series, chose the relevant articles, organized the book according to themes, and drove the project.

We worked with our incredible illustrator Kevin Gillespie to bring these chapters to life. Kevin has absorbed positive psychology from his wife, Eleanor Chin, a 2008 Penn MAPP graduate and another author for the online publication.

Big thanks to each author, Martin Seligman, Kathryn Britton, Kevin Gillespie, and Robert Emmons, a pre-eminent author about gratitude whose work inspired many of the chapters of this book.

Senia Maymin, 2010

Two Invitations

First, we invite you to visit the online discussion area for this book to add your questions and stories:
www.PositivePsychologyNews.com/book/gratitude

Second, we invite you to visit *Positive Psychology News Daily* (**www.PositivePsychologyNews.com**)
and to subscribe to email updates
(**www.PositivePsychologyNews.com/DailyEmails**).

Join the community! We provide a frequent boost of research-based knowledge about happiness, productivity, and gratitude.

Table of Contents

Illustrations

The internal illustrations were drawn by Kevin Gillespie. For information about Kevin, see the last page of the book.

The photograph on the cover was taken by Edward Britton stalking a visitor to his butterfly garden.

INTRODUCTION

Gratitude is many things.

Gratitude is awareness of benefits that we are not responsible for ourselves. We are not entitled to them, but they still exist, to our good fortune.

Gratitude is a momentary positive emotion. Research shows that positive emotions like gratitude, joy, contentment, amusement, interest, and love can broaden our ranges of behavior, making us more creative and open to new possibilities. They also help us build durable resources such as resilience and social connections.

Gratitude is a character strength recognized around the world and across time. Some people are stronger at feeling and expressing gratitude than others. It is possible to increase this character strength with intentional effort.

Gratitude is a moral motive that affects our behavior. By noticing the things that others do for us, we reinforce our will and energy to do good for others.

Gratitude is a habit that can be cultivated with intentional activity yielding many benefits.

How do we know about gratitude? It has received considerable attention in positive psychology research.

Positive psychology is an empirical discipline. Researchers formulate ideas and test them. They work to discover the difference between common wisdom and common mistakes. How well do certain approaches really work in practice with large populations? What tools or techniques really work?

Those of us working in applied positive psychology are concerned with another question. How do we make the growing body of empirical research available to the general population so that it can make a difference in people's lives?

The purpose of this little book is to make findings in positive psychology accessible to people who do not want to read research papers, but still have a curiosity about what research tells us. It conveys the messages with stories, examples, and suggested actions that are immediately useful.

This little book is based on articles published in the online news source, *Positive Psychology News Daily*. It contains different points of view from 16 authors who live in 3 different continents. Each chapter is followed by questions, challenges, and suggestions submitted by readers of the online article. These discussions display the community feeling that surrounds the online publication.

PART I: THE VALUE OF GRATITUDE

Gratitude improves the quality of life.

Building habits of gratitude is one of the most effective ways to increase well-being. Psychologist Sonya Lyubomirsky describes the expression of gratitude as "a metastrategy for achieving happiness."

Jen Hausmann's *Three Good Things* offers a child's eye view of purposefully looking for reasons to be grateful every day. To put positive psychology concepts into practice as she learned them, Jen began a bedtime tradition with her 7-year-old son, Jonah, of sharing three good things that happened during the day. Curious about what her son thought of this new tradition, Jen decided to interview him. Jonah wanted his mother to share their positive feelings about gratitude. She includes an occasional translation from kid language into adult language because Jonah wanted to be sure that people got it.

Sherri Fisher's *Thanks to Gratitude!* explains some of the benefits of gratitude, particularly in the context of our most important relationships. People who regularly express gratitude tend to have better sleep, better relationships, and better moods. She describes the development of gratitude in children, and ties gratitude to experiencing and expressing kindness toward others.

Chapter 1 Three Good Things by Jen Hausmann

Jen Hausmann, MAPP '06, works as a project and communications manager for David's Bridal, a nationwide retail chain for bridal and special occasion apparel. Introducing applications of positive psychology into a corporate retail environment is one of her key interests.

For a year, I studied cutting-edge concepts in positive psychology in the MAPP program at Penn. One study in particular intrigued me: participants were instructed to notice three things each evening that went well that day and why they went well. Although this experiment lasted only one week, *six months later* the participants were significantly higher in happiness than the control group. *"Gratitude?"* I thought, *"Really?"*

I found the best way to experience positive psychology was to test the theories at home. So I started doing a variation of the gratitude exercise every night with my little boy, Jonah. Right before bedtime, we would sit together and think of three positive or happy things that happened during the day. He quickly called it *Three Good Things.* I am not sure how many days it took, but it quickly became a habit, and I now firmly believe that this is one of the most powerful happiness exercises and one of the easiest to perform. Now Jonah reminds me if I forget to be thankful for the good things that happen each day. Prior to studying positive psychology, I would have been skeptical about the utility of cultivating gratitude. Only a few months later, it became a bedtime ritual.

Seeing the effect of *Three Good Things* on my son inspired great interest in the impact that positive psychology can have on children at a very young age. Curious about what Jonah, a very typical 7-year-old boy, gets out of doing *Three Good Things*, I decided to ask. I continue to be amazed by the insights of young children before they learn to be skeptical. Jonah already clearly has a handle on how gratitude works. Here are some of our questions and answers, with adult translations when necessary. The translations were requested and confirmed by Jonah to make sure grown-ups "get it."

Bedtime Blessings

Mom: What do you think of our bedtime tradition of talking about three good things?

Jonah: Umm, I like it. It's like, you know...good to share good stuff...Why? Don't you like it? (I responded "Yes.")

Mom: Why do you think we like doing three good things?

Jonah: Because you get to share your day with the people that you love, and the things you share are probably things you'd like to do again. Usually, you share something that either makes you happy or you had fun with. And it feels good to be happy. I mean, you might have an amazing good thing that you liked. And the thing that you liked is probably something that you found, did, helped someone, or felt loved about.

Mom: Why do you think it feels good to talk about our good things?

Jonah: Maybe because you might have something that wasn't fun so if you talk about the good things, well, the bad things, you won't think about any more.

Adult translation: Focusing on the positive can detract from the power of the negative.

Mom: How do you choose your good things?

Jonah: The weird thing is, you might not have done a good thing or had fun, so you can share something that you think someone else had fun with... because that would be good, to have something good happen to someone you love, too...

Adult translation: Our happiness can be enhanced by the increased happiness of those around us.

Mom: Is it always easy to think of three good things?

Jonah: You might get stressed because you might not be able to get one out. Oh, but if it was Saturday or Sunday, your parents could help you share one. Because Saturday and Sunday are home days so your parents will probably know what you did because you were probably on vacation with them or outside or watching TV or reading a book with your parents. Or, if you're somebody that doesn't have any good things, and your parents can't help you think of one, you can share it with your friends who might think of something and you could brainstorm.

Adult translation: Sometimes it's important to have people around who remind us of the good things we have.

Mom: Do you think it would be good to teach other people how to do three good things?

Jonah: I think it would, but you shouldn't just, like, come in and stuff...You'd have to let them pick whether it was something they'd want to do. They might want to do other things or have another feeling.

Adult translation: You can't force other people to be grateful for what they have, but, you can offer opportunities to share.

Mom: Do you think it would be just as good to talk about more than three things? Why do we pick three?

Jonah: There might be like a thousand or a million things you liked that you did today, but you'll only choose three, and those will be your best.

I think it is just the right amount because you don't have to add or keep track too much because it's only three. What I mean is, if you have three, you might have one favorite, then the second favorite then the third. If there were more, then you might change your mind all the time because you would have your most favorite thing confused and then you'd have to keep it all straight in your head. So three is good, actually.

Adult translation: Four would be one too many. Sometimes less is more.

Final (and my personal favorite) closing comment...

You know what would be cool, if you asked your old teacher, like from that college thing you did, if you could publish this and kids would want to read it.

Jonah James Hausmann (Age 7)

Discussion

Senia: Reading this makes me so happy! Thank you, Jen! Thank you, Jonah!

It's just so real and fun. My parents used to say when I was a kid that kids know the real depth of things. They know what things really are, the truth behind things. I see that here.

Jonah, I especially like your point about how you shouldn't just come in and make someone do the exercise – only if they want to, and they might have ideas about how they enjoy doing the exercise. Finally, I call this "three great things" also just like your "three good things." Thanks, you joint authors!

Kathryn: Your experience with Jonah reminds me of a friend who complained that she didn't know how to have fun. I suggested that she ask her 9-year-old son. When she did, he wrote her a manual of things to do — many of which were doing things with him.

Thank you for bringing us Jonah's wisdom. Jonah, thanks for sharing.

Jeff: My wife is a guidance counselor at the elementary level. She and I swapped email correspondence with positive psychology professors, Jon Haidt and Karen Reivich (among others), about how to tap into resiliency and happiness exercises for impressionable younger ages. Isn't prevention at least as powerful if not more so than cure?

Well, no one has an answer except social modeling. Show the monkey and see the monkey dance like you! I can't wait for the big brains to delve into this elementary topic. You are doing some extremely important action research!

Sharon: Loved hearing about the three good things that happened in a day. I wish I had known about three good things when my kids were young. If I ever have grandkids, I will tell my children about it so they can share it with their children.

Chapter 2 Thanks to Gratitude! By Sherri Fisher

Sherri Fisher, MAPP '06, M.Ed., combines 25 years experience in PK-12 education with positive psychology to uncover engaged learning and working solutions for both individuals and organizations. She is a principal of three education-related businesses.

Did you know that over two thirds of happy experiences come from relationships? Gratitude is the feeling we experience when we perceive ourselves as the receivers of intentional gifts from others. Very happy people have happier memories of events and have more highly satisfying relationships with friends, romantic partners, and family members.

Kindness, Gratitude and Happiness

Compared to unhappy people, happy people feel more grateful when they receive kindnesses. They are more motivated to be kind and more likely to recognize kindness in others.

Gratitude and Human Development

Gratitude building starts early. The social skills that we teach children help develop it. Very young children can learn that people are grateful for socially desired behaviors, and this can make them willing to behave better most of the time.

In studies with grade school children, those ten years or older expressed gratitude more than 80% of the time compared to a tiny fraction of six-year-olds. If your children don't like writing thank you letters, stick with it. It may be that they don't enjoy the writing or the gift, but it may also be that they just aren't feeling that grateful — yet.

A Bouquet of Kindness

In surveys of school-aged populations, girls tend to be most grateful for interpersonal relationships, and boys tend to be most grateful for material possessions. Further, the indebtedness that some boys feel when a kindness is bestowed upon them may actually keep them from feeling gratitude because they want to avoid a sense of obligation that can feel like guilt.

In a lab setting, people who were induced to feel grateful felt higher life satisfaction and lower desire for more material goods. When participants were induced to feel envious of others' possessions, however, they experienced higher materialism. It's hard to feel grateful, of course, when you focus on people's stuff instead of them. Remember this when you are being bombarded (or stealthily seduced) by advertising.

Gratitude and Relationship Building

Adolescents who are more grateful tend to have higher well-being, optimism, and social support. Gratitude promotes relationship formation and maintenance. When people are kind to us, it shows that they are responding to our whole self, our likes or dislikes, our needs, and our preferences. Gratitude makes both the giver and the receiver happy. Research with young women shows that the more effort they perceive went into kind acts, the more gratitude they generally feel. Kindness and gratitude encourage people to create meaningful experiences for others.

Gratitude is Beneficial

Feeling grateful before bed leads to improved sleep and a greater sense of refreshment upon waking. Since good sleep quality reduces daytime distraction, feeling grateful may contribute to better study and work outcomes.

The experience of gratitude prevents us from doing things that would be destructive to our relationships. It helps us experience happiness, hope, pride, and optimism. Gratitude leads to more frequent positive moods, a sense of self-actualization, and a sense of community. Gratitude is related to school success and satisfaction.

You Can Experience More Gratitude

Three easy and effective ways to experience more gratitude include:

- Write a letter of gratitude to someone and deliver it in person to share your feelings.
- Keep a gratitude journal.
- Keep a "counting your kindnesses" journal. Noticing the ways you are kind makes you both happier and more likely to do even more kind things that set up the positive relationship cycle.

Make yourself happier and make the world a better place. As you go into the world today, remember to appreciate and reciprocate!

Discussion

Marcial: I am married to one of the most grateful people I've ever known, and I can testify to two benefits you mention in your excellent article: she sleeps like a baby and has a very high ratio of positive to negative emotions. The only problem is that I am not as grateful as she is, and oftentimes I find myself awake in the middle of the night. Counting sheep or anything else doesn't help, so I am going to follow your advice and count my blessings instead.

Sherri: I have been trying the late-night blessings approach myself. I'm glad you are married to someone who is so grateful. You must bring lots of value to the marriage, too. Does being thanked make you feel obligated or do you want to reciprocate?

Marcial: Good question, Sherri. I believe I am more of the reciprocating kind of guy.

Denise Q.: It's lovely to be reminded how important gratitude is to our relationships. As regards children and gratitude letters – yes, we can make them stick to it. Alternatively we can try to find out how each child naturally wants to express gratitude and encourage him or her to do it that way. We could ask them to think of a time something happened that they felt really grateful for, and ask what they felt like doing then. We know very little about how children of different ages spontaneously express gratitude. I'm a big fan of asking them.

Sherri: Your suggestions are spot on. I agree about finding what works naturally for kids and working from there. I was following the line of thought that gratitude, at least as it is thought of by adults, is not yet developed in young kids.

Marc: I noticed you listed the "gratitude journal" at the end of the article. We kept a gratitude journal as part of an exercise for a class I attended. What troubled me was that I had a very difficult time coming up with things that I was grateful for. Part of this was because I tend to attribute every good thing throughout the day to an action of my own. In the text we are using for that class, it states that this is a common issue among people.

Sherri: Try priming or reframing to experience more gratitude, for example by noticing random or undeserved good things that happen to you. It might be a beautiful day, or a particularly attentive waiter, or someone letting you cut into a line of heavy traffic.

I ask my students to consider these three questions for their gratitude journals. This is a way to integrate strengths, savoring, and gratitude.
–What happened? (Turn on your noticing/appreciating gear.)
–What was good about it? (Why did you think/feel it was good? Can you connect it to your strengths? Values?)
–Why did it happen? (Can you make it happen again? Or is it something special to savor that might be a once-in-a-lifetime event?)

Chris: I am currently conducting a research project on people's ability to take in gratitude from others. When people can take in gratitude, the impact is immense, but I find people really struggle to experience gratitude expressed by others.

Johnny: Another way to increase your feelings of gratitude is to change your assumptions. For example, I believe that if it weren't for empathic and kind people in the world, life would be much harder because the natural universe is mostly harsh and unforgiving. Also I believe that no one in this world, not even my parents, owes me anything at all. So I feel grateful for anything anyone does for me.

I am curious about why the research shows the feeling of indebtedness reduces the feeling of gratitude. As an American male, I definitely do feel a sense of owing someone who does something kind for me. It's a desire to keep things fair. Yet for some reason this does not diminish my thankfulness.

Sherri: Do you suppose that in collectivist cultures the importance of honor and filial piety would have a big effect on whether someone feels gratitude versus indebtedness to return favors?

Johnny: I neglected to mention that I am bi-cultural (Taiwanese American), and while I've been here since I was one, I also retain parts of my parent's culture. This includes my exposure to Buddhism, which definitely influenced my perception regarding gratitude. The version of Buddhism I was exposed to had a great emphasis on possessing gratitude for all things. I can see how that would modify the indebtedness to include feelings of gratitude as well.

PART II: GRATITUDE PRACTICES

Part II explores specific ways to increase the day-to-day experience of gratitude.

In *Building Gratitude*, Kathryn Britton describes six different ways to become more thankful. Most of them involve changing where we focus attention and how we interpret the events going on around us. She even found a way to be grateful when she tripped over a tree root and fell.

In *Facing Surgery with Gratitude*, Miriam Akhtar answers her own questions, "Is there anything positive to be extracted from the experience of surgery? Can we use positive psychology to prepare for going under the surgeon's knife?" She uses four concepts that she learned in her study of positive psychology, including a focus on gratitude. She found that surgery gave her many opportunities to be grateful.

In *Gratitude in a Time of Downsizing*, Sean Doyle tells the story of a worker on the verge of burnout, passed over for promotion, and living in fear of downsizing. Then the worker started keeping a gratitude journal. Find out what kinds of things he put in his journal and how the journal changed his attitudes and his life.

Chapter 3 Building Gratitude by Kathryn Britton

 *Kathryn Britton, MAPP '06, is a coach, adjunct instructor at the University of Maryland, and associate editor of Positive Psychology News Daily. She works toward positive workplaces where people can be highly productive and satisfied with work that they find meaningful.*

There are many facets of work and life in general that we do not control. But we can increase our control over our responses to them. One way to raise our overall level of wellbeing even in the face of trouble and stress is to practice and grow stronger at being grateful.

Practicing gratitude is an intentional activity that can make a real and ongoing difference in chronic happiness levels. Research indicates that people who conduct certain gratitude exercises are healthier and feel better about their lives, make more progress toward goals, are more optimistic, and are more likely to help others than people in control groups.

So how do we increase the level of gratitude we experience in our jobs and our lives? Here are a few suggestions:

Pay attention to good things, large and small. This often requires intentional thought because we tend to be more easily aware of bad things than good things. For example, I have a friend in his 80's with arthritis in his hands. He becomes aware of it whenever he knocks something over or has trouble picking something up. I suggested that whenever he finds himself saying, "My poor crippled hands," that he follow it with "My magnificent legs that let me walk every day without cane or walker." That does not mean ignoring the painful. It means balancing it with occasional thoughts of how lucky we are to have so many working parts! We have to work a little to give the positive thoughts space in our brains.

Pay attention to bad things that are avoided. I recently tripped over a tree root and fell flat on my face during a practice hike to get ready for our trip to the mountains. When I picked myself up, I was very grateful to have only a deep bruise on my thigh, no broken bones. It will take a while for the gorgeous 8-inch bruise to go away, but I can still hike. Thank goodness!

Grateful for What Did Not Happen

Practice downward comparisons. That means thinking about how things could be worse, or were worse, or are worse for someone else. I don't particularly like the idea of making myself feel more grateful by thinking of others who are worse off than I am. But it doesn't have to be interpersonal. You can use downward comparison by remembering your own times of adversity or being aware of adversity avoided.

The poet, Robert Pollock, said it thus: "Sorrows remembered sweeten present joy." Here's a work example. I have two friends who recently moved into the same department in the same company. One is relieved and happy because the situation seems so much better than before. The other is dissatisfied because he feels the team worked better on the old job. The first has an easy time with downward contrast. The second will have to work a little harder to find reasons to be grateful.

Establish regular times to focus on being grateful. Gratitude is a character strength that can be enhanced with practice. So practice at bedtime, on arising, or during meals.

When facing a loss or a difficult task or situation, **remind yourself to be grateful both for what you haven't lost** *and for the strengths and opportunities that arise from facing difficulties.* Researchers found that benefit-seeking and benefit-remembering are linked to psychological and physical health. Benefit-seeking involves choosing to focus on the positive aspects of the situation and avoiding the feeling of being a victim.

Elicit and reinforce gratitude in the people around you. Negative moods are catching, but positive ones can be as well. The character Pollyanna helped other people see the benefits in their situations by teaching them the Glad Game. Sometimes, having someone else see what is good in your own life makes it visible to you.

Gratitude is a character strength admired around the globe. To increase gratitude, a good first step is to notice the good things that happen to us, large and small. These practices can help us take fewer blessings for granted.

Discussion

Senia: I really appreciate this article because I have a tepid attitude towards gratitude, probably because it often seems so general to me. I much prefer specifics.

I REALLY like your suggestion about downward comparison even though at first glance it may appear strange. Research really does show that this is extremely valuable as a coping technique and a mood booster. I especially like your suggestion that it doesn't have to be a downward social comparison of you versus the Joneses. It can be you versus a previous version of you.

I really like your concrete suggestions here because often people – including me – can imagine being grateful and thankful for those things that DO exist, but it's harder to be grateful for those yucky things avoided. And that's why your story about just having a bruise and being able to continue hiking is a great example.

Sevgi: I like your suggestions. They are so realistic and applicable. The person in the street in my country, Turkey, sees positive psychology as a kind of Pollyanna game, meaning ignoring reality. Is that true? Not really. Thinking positively can be Pollyanna's Glad Game. Using the Glad Game, people can easily recognize what they have in their hands and can easily rescue themselves from downward spirals.

I agree with all your suggestions. They all work. We should teach your suggestions to educators. Then our children can easily learn to think positively by their socialization process.

Chapter 4 Facing Surgery with Gratitude by Miriam Akhtar

 *Miriam Akhtar, MAPP '09, University of East London, is a positive psychologist in practice as a trainer and coach. She researches and writes about positive psychology interventions for depression and is the co-presenter of the audio program, The Happiness Training Plan.*

"... But just to be on the safe side, we'll need to operate."

Those are words many of us will have to deal with at some point in our lives. They happened to me, and I found myself facing surgery for the first time. As I contemplated how the surgeon would extract a suspect part from my body, I wondered if there was anything positive to be extracted from the experience of undergoing surgery. Can we use positive psychology to prepare for going under the surgeon's knife?

It turns out the answer was a resounding yes. I left the hospital on a big high and not just from the cocktail of drugs. My first experience of the operating table turned out to be surprisingly positive and led to a torrent of gratitude. So here I offer my tips for surgical well-being.

#1) Build up motivation for getting well. Motivation comes from three basic needs: feeling competent, strong relationships with others, and having autonomy. My autonomy was significant as my procedure is usually carried out under general anesthesia. Since I have a history of allergic reactions (including anaphylactic shock), you can understand why I'd prefer to be conscious and able to communicate in the event of having an adverse reaction. It was a relief when the anesthetist gave me the **autonomy** to choose a local anesthesia even though it was going against the norm.

This acknowledged my **competence** in making the best decision for my body and helped to calm my nerves before the operation.

Surgery was a time of vulnerability when **relatedness** really counted. Feeling fragile, I found this a good time to lean on friends and family for support. A good model for relatedness came from the nurses who soothed me on the way to the operating room. It did make me laugh when, just as the surgeon wielded his scalpel, the anesthetic nurse attempted to distract me with that old cliché of the hairdressing salon, "And where are you going on holiday this year?" Nice try. It didn't work!

#2) Use Your Strengths

Finding new ways of using your strengths can lead to lasting increases in happiness. Surgery provided a new way, and I found all of my top character strengths came into play naturally on the day. OK, here I have to confess that my top strength, Curiosity, was also behind my desire to have the procedure done under local anesthesia. I wasn't going to miss the chance to nose around a real operating theater.

My Appreciation of Beauty strength may have been facilitated by the anesthetic – those bright white lights carry a hint of heavenly blue, accented by the sky blue of the surgeon's scrubs and the turquoise of the sterile sheet which was placed in front of my eyes so I couldn't watch what was going on (boo!). My Love of Learning and Social Intelligence strengths helped me set about bonding with the surgeon. I had a chance to gain an insight into the operation and one of the highest status jobs around. During the operation, I found Creativity kicking in as I imagined writing about one of the more surreal experiences of my life.

I came out of the operating room to a chorus of praise for my strength in making it through the operation fully conscious, which put me on a high that lingered for weeks.

#3) Choose Optimism

I actively used optimism as an aid in recovery. Optimistic patients tend to experience less distress pre-surgery and greater relief, resilience, and long-lasting life satisfaction post-surgery. From the moment I received the news about the operation, I chose to believe that my body was already healed and distracted myself by focusing on how I was going to experience surgery positively. My healing was rapid and I made a gentle return to work 48 hours later. When I went back for the biopsy report, I got the result I hoped for, the all-clear. I believe my choice of an optimistic perspective helped create the reality that occurred.

#4) Practice Gratitude

Gratitude has tended to be something I've done dryly in my head in the past, but having surgery unleashed a flood of heart-felt appreciation with all the accompanying positive emotions. The gift in surgery is that it presents you with many natural opportunities for gratitude. Being confronted with the reality of mortality renews appreciation for life itself. There's fresh gratitude for the love of those who support you during this vulnerable time and appreciation for the skill and care of the medics in helping you back to health. Truly a case of surgical well-being.

Sleep After Practicing Gratitude

Discussion

Dave S.: Thanks for sharing this experience. If positive psychology doesn't matter in facing real challenges (and opportunities) in our lives, then why bother? You turned a challenge into an opportunity!

Chapter 5 Gratitude in a Time of Downsizing by Sean Doyle

 *A poet and lawyer, Sean Doyle, MAPP '07, JD, offers strengths-based consulting for organizations and acts as an advisor and confidant to people about their personal sources of joy, about how they want to live their lives, and about how they find meaning in life and work.*

"It was inevitable: the burnt scent of over-warmed coffee always reminded him of the fate of unrequited devotion." Paraphrase of the first line of *Love in the Time of Cholera* by Gabriel Garcia Marquez.

The Disengagement Trap

Florentino is in his mid-forties, and he has worked for a Fortune 500 company for the last ten years. For the first six, he worked hard, stayed late into the evenings, and brought files home on the weekends. However after several small events that caused him to question his role in the organization, he was passed over for a promotion. While neither corrosive nor hostile, he always knew that his work environment was far from supportive. No one acknowledged his work or talked with him about his progress. Missing out on the promotion was the final act that broke the stamina of someone who had been a committed and loyal employee. While he continued to do the minimum necessary for his job, by all measures, Florentino was disengaged and unhappy.

Florentino is not alone. According to polls by the Gallup organization, 55% of the U.S. workforce is disengaged in their jobs, and 16% are actively disengaged, for a total of 71%. In addition to this picture of mass individual drudgery, Gallup estimates that having 16% of the workforce actively disengaged costs American businesses roughly $350 billion each year. A country with a GDP this size would rank as the 28th largest economy in the world, ahead of the nations of South Africa, Finland, and the United Arab Emirates (UAE).

As the economy softened and opportunities to find jobs became limited, Florentino felt trapped. He began to worry that his disillusionment would be noticed in a time of downsizing. While he did not like his job, he needed it. Florentino began to feel desperate.

Gratitude as a Way Out of the Trap

While Florentino ultimately had to decide whether he wanted to stay with his company, it was clear that the first thing he had to do was stop sabotaging himself with his negative thoughts about his job. Florentino began to keep a work-centered gratitude journal.

Keeping a gratitude journal involves setting aside time each day to write down several things that went well, or for which you are otherwise grateful. It is better to write something new each day. Some people also write what contributed to a good event, why it occurred, or what made an item particularly special. Studies show that keeping a gratitude journal has long-lasting positive effects on life satisfaction and well-being.

Entries in Florentino's Gratitude Journal

Florentino kept his journal at work, and focused exclusively on things related to his job. The first items were easy and obvious: "I am grateful that I have a job that allows me to support my family," and "I don't have to ask anyone's permission to take sick leave."

But after a few days, it got a little harder. He started becoming aware of things that had previously slipped beneath notice. "People will change direction on projects based on my input," and "Dave stopped me in the parking lot and told me that one of the clients spoke really highly of me."

Keeping a Gratitude Journal

After just a few days the resentment he felt at work dissipated. He had always been professional and friendly to people at work, but now he was taking interest in his coworkers on more personal levels. They responded to him. Journal entries included things like, "Thomas [someone with whom he had never really gotten along] told me it was the anniversary of his wife's death. He had never shared anything personal with me before. All of a sudden he seemed much more human."

Within a few weeks, he was seeking new projects and looking for ways that he could contribute. While he still did not love his job, he began to recognize how he could affect others in positive ways every single day, and the work began to give him greater levels of satisfaction.

Reframing the events of our lives in positive ways and including a glimmer of gratitude, we increase our belief that the world makes sense. Then we feel more grounded and at peace.

Four Months Later

Florentino no longer writes in the journal every day. Now he adds an entry about once a week. However this March, four months after he started his journal, Florentino received a promotion. The new job was a better fit than the one he lost. It gives him the chance to do exactly those things that first drew him to the job.

When asked about his new job and his feelings for his company, "And how long do you think you can keep up this coming and going?" Florentino had his answer ready. "Forever," he said.

Author's Note: The title, first line and last paragraph of this article paraphrase the title, beginning, and ending of Gabriel Garcia Marquez's novel, *Love in the Time of Cholera*. Further, the name of the individual has been changed to that of the character in the novel that lived the "fate of unrequited love."

Discussion

Kathryn: Thank you for Florentino's story. It makes the general ideas about gratitude come alive. The specific instances of things he found to write in his log are great ways to prime the pump.

Sean: Thanks Kathryn! As I worked with Florentino, I felt motivated as I saw him change and succeed.

Wayne: Ultimately at the end of the day you have to work out what works for each individual and not rely on generalizations.

Imagine a scenario where you get someone to do a gratitude exercise and it doesn't work for him or her. How would he or she feel? Could it have the opposite effect?

The other thing to consider is that often coaches will extrapolate their values onto others – I'm betting that gratitude might be one of your top five strengths.

Sean: Thanks the feedback, Wayne. I always welcome your input.

I agree that "at the end of the day you have to work out what works for each individual and not rely on generalizations."

That is consistent with practicing positive psychology. The science does not promote a one-size-fits-all approach. However, what a great reminder of what can happen as this material is sent out for public consumption. I know gratitude journals do not work for everyone, but I did not point this out in the article. You make a very valuable and important point. If we are not attentive to this fact, it undermines both the science and our ability to affect others positively.

(Oh and personally gratitude did not appear in my top five character strengths.)

PART III: AN APPRECIATIVE EYE

So many times, people look around at the world primed to see what is going wrong. Part III explores a different approach, looking around expecting to find things to appreciate.

The way we talk affects what we and our hearers experience. In *Appreciative Dialogue*, Angus Skinner pictures life as a soup of discourse that can be flavored with appreciation.

People serve us in many ways. We can take service for granted and only notice it when it is poor. Or we can pay attention to the invisible hands that make life smooth and pleasant. In *Appreciating Service*, Yee-Ming Tan talks about responding positively to service in a hotel and how much additional pleasure she received as a result.

Gratitude is not a luxury limited to fortunate people. In *Everyone Can Appreciate*, Nicholas Hall describes an outpouring of gratitude that he observed at an outpatient facility for adults recovering from prolonged psychiatric illness.

In *Divorce: From Anger to Appreciation*, Kirsten Cronlund describes four techniques she used to change her view of her divorce and bring sparkle back into her life.

In Praise of Praise includes Timothy So's musings about giving and getting praise. He wonders why praise is so seldom used. He reflects on what he learned from someone who gave him masterful praise. He also considers the difference that effective praise could make in organizations.

Chapter 6 Appreciative Dialogue by Angus Skinner

 *Angus Skinner, MAPP '06, works in his beloved and beautiful Scotland as a visiting Professor at the University of Strathclyde.*

We swim in the soup of constant discourse. Our lives are flavored by the content and meaning of our conversations.

Say you are driving your child to school, and I cut you off in traffic (dead annoying). If you say "Men drivers – all the bxxx same," then your child has learned that this problem is pervasive (all men) and permanent (no hope).

If you say "Agh, I wonder what is wrong with that guy today?" then your child has learned this is a temporary problem (today) and limited to one man (me).

Discourse like this goes on all the time – in offices, families, parties, and in the street. Our chatter and its meaning is so ever-present, it often becomes submerged below awareness. But this soup we swim in affects us.

It is easy enough to create a culture of depression. As humans we seem to be experts. Even when our natural skills in this seem to fail us, we can call up ancient as well as modern manuals. Most cultures have norms and sayings that warn against too much enjoyment or success — they are like safety valves. They protect us from too much hope. I can't blame us; sorrow, pain, and death are unavoidable in life.

But we have to be aware of the unintended effects of negative discourse. We should stop passively swimming in our soup and step forward as cooks in the kitchen. Intentionally, we can flavor life with appreciation.

A culture of appreciation creates upward spirals in relationships and performance. Healthy family relationships appear to require a 5:1 ratio in positive to negative interactions, while work seems to require a 3:1 ratio. Seems we will put up with more negativity at work. Well, we're paid for it.

Soup of Discourse

I believe creating a culture of appreciation is mainly about listening, whether in organizations or in personal relationships. If people don't think you are listening, they cannot hear what you say. Listen. And be creative.

Whatever your situation, you can build an upward spiral. The discourse, the conversations, and the body language are all crucial to creating a culture of appreciation.

Enjoy making your own soup!

Discussion

Senia: Angus, I think you are so right – it's those quick, non-mindful moments when we can get into so much trouble. Just the off-the-cuff comments that we can make – within hearing range of kids, colleagues, friends, and even ourselves!

Christine: I agree with you that a culture of appreciation is a good place to start — in business and personally. Not always easy, but it makes a huge difference.

Sherri: I love visual metaphors and the soup one is great. It speaks to the point that we have a lot of choice about what goes in the recipe.

Research helps us know what works in general, thus narrowing the range of choices to ones that have been shown to work. Research is like a menu of tasty meals. There are "restaurants" for mindfulness, resilience, building positive emotion to name a few. Here's to a great soup menu!

Chapter 7 Appreciating Service by Yee-Ming Tan

 *Yee-Ming Tan, MAPP '07, provides executive coaching services to senior executives in Asia. Recent clients include Standard Chartered Bank, Mead Johnson, and Microsoft. She also publishes RippleCards, a tool for people who choose to cultivate greater well-being.*

I find restaurants a great place to practice being positive, and very often, I receive great service in return. I've concluded that positive customer behavior begets positive service. Here's what I do in restaurants:

1. Flash a big smile to the waiter or waitress
2. Establish eye contact
3. Call the waiter or waitress by name
4. Express my appreciation for the service
5. Show my interest in him or her

Thinking about appreciation, I recall a wonderful episode from my vacation on a private rain forest island in Malaysia.

On the first morning at breakfast, my partner and I were lucky to get a table in the garden, surrounded by lush tropical plants and a wandering peacock! I noticed a waiter, Jonathan, who stood out from the rest of the staff because of his genuine smile.

Engaging him in conversation, I learned a bit about his story. Jonathan, a Nepali, came to work in Malaysia 4 years ago. Because of this conversation, we established a connection as individuals beyond the buyer and seller relationship. My partner and I had a great morning enjoying our leisurely breakfast being looked after by Jonathan.

Breakfast in Malaysia

On the second morning, we had the same table, and Jonathan again looked after us. I brought my own mango, a big juicy Indian mango, that morning. Jonathan came over and offered to have the kitchen prepare it for us. It was so kind of him to do this. I made a mental note to write to the hotel general manager about such outstanding service.

On our third and final morning there, Jonathan surprised us with a plate of mango on the house! It was a special treat because mango was not on the menu. He also packed us some snacks for our ferry trip home.

The smile, the attention, the acknowledgment, the appreciation, the interest from our side brought out the best in Jonathan, who in turn gave us the best gift – a high point and a great ending experience for our vacation.

Discussion

Steve: That's a great point. Our attitude either attracts or repels positivity or negativity. It's important to keep these principles in mind with all our interactions. Also, it's important to think of these principles as a way of being, versus as a means to get what we want. The law of indirect effort states that we must give without intention of receiving, in order to receive.

Yee-Ming: Thanks for picking up on this point – giving without intention of receiving. Authentic positivity is a way of being. I do it as a personal practice, without considering how the other person might react. I certainly do not get this special experience every time I go into a restaurant. However I would say I tend to have more good service than bad service.

Chapter 8 Everyone Can Appreciate by Nicholas Hall

 *Nicholas Hall, MAPP '06, is manager of the Stanford University Graduate School of Business Behavioral Lab. He consults on worker satisfaction and engagement, and sits on the ad-advisory board of Omnirisk Management Tools. His research focuses on work satisfaction, character strengths, and positive psychology.*

I was recently invited to speak at a support facility for adults recovering from the prolonged effects of psychiatric illness. The Bridge House offers a number of services including a work-ordered day, employment and housing programs, social activities, educational opportunities, and personalized recovery oriented goal planning and case management. They also provide outreach support for the homeless in the area.

When I entered the cafeteria where I was going to give the talk, I was unsure how people would respond. This was a group with real mental and emotional, not to mention personal, difficulties. Could they relate to what I was going to say? I thought that I would at least have to simplify the material on the fly. Would they participate?

Once the talk on gratitude was underway, the group was immediately responsive and engaged. I had to force myself to keep going because I got so many responses to my questions.

After a time, I finally got to describe the gratitude letter and visit. In this classic intervention, a person thinks of someone he or she has never thanked properly, writes a thank-you letter, and then delivers it in person, reading it out loud to the person being thanked. I asked for volunteers to mention someone who was important to them, and then to tell us what the person did and how it made them feel. A woman spoke up and pointed to the young woman intern at the end of the table. The speaker said, "She's leaving tomorrow. She has been very important to us. She is a very nice and sweet person."

The flood gates were opened. Each person around the room was eager to describe the positive attributes of the intern and how these attributes contributed to them personally and to Bridge House collectively.

"She is very helpful."

"She is so sweet and kind."

"She makes me feel good."

"She knows where the need is and responds right away."

"She helped me quit smoking."

The intern was in tears. Gratitude permeated the room, and it was focused on one person. Every face was lit up and smiling. The intern tearfully thanked everyone.

Applause

Is Gratitude for Everyone?

We sometimes act as if ideas like gratitude are only for normally functioning individuals with clear cognitive abilities, not those suffering from depression or having difficulty functioning day-to-day.

I can tell you from my experience at Bridge House that even those recovering from serious mental illness respond amazingly well to ideas like gratitude. They can truly benefit from exploring their character strengths. They can feel the strength of these interventions, and they most certainly can see the importance of gratitude in their lives. Working on happiness is important for them to stay afloat in their lives.

More than a year ago, a man named Lionel Ketchian, "a regular businessman" as he puts it, began giving weekly talks on happiness at Bridge House. He is responsible for introducing general positive psychology principles to the population there. He tells me that within a year, this withdrawn and anti-social group has turned into a set of engaged and empowered individuals. The staff even report enjoying working there more.

To say that this place is a much needed haven of support for those in this struggling part of Bridgeport is an understatement. The Bridge House workers are indeed angels for this community in need. I, too, am grateful for having a chance to contribute something small to a community that has built so much for itself.

Discussion

Angus: Great work Nick – I especially love the way the flood gates opened. And then everyone, if I read you right, was energized!

I absolutely agree that positive psychology is applicable for all. I see it more like learning to play tennis or golf – we all learn from the best. It is also true that sick is sick, and there are things you can change and things you can't.

Atlanta: Congratulations on being adventurous. I see a great use for positive psychology with populations with problems. My interest is in using it with people who have addictions in order to strengthen their recovery. 12 step programs have been advocating gratitude for years.

Phyllis: I work at Bridge House, where Nick did his presentation. There are generally 60 people who have lunch at our Clubhouse model of psychiatric rehabilitation, and of those approximately 15 or 20 choose to regularly attend our monthly Happiness Lunch. This self-selected group is like a sponge for positive psychology! I really hope that Nick will return and become part of our ongoing quest for happiness. The participants are poor, inner city adults, all with an Axis 1 diagnosis...and they are all so receptive to ideas for ways to feel better. Thanks Nick!

Chapter 9 Divorce: From Anger to Appreciation by Kirsten Cronlund

 *Kirsten Cronlund, MAPP '08, is a founder of Lemonade from Lemons: Divorce Coaching, Workshops and Seminars. She is committed to helping others navigate the rough waters of di- divorce with resilience. She is now serving as the Director of Bryn Athyn Church School.*

There seems to be little in divorce that is sparkling and fragrant. Hopes and dreams crash and burn, the financial future is uncertain, and angry words are often flung in an effort to protect tender hearts.

But if you can only lift your eyes above the immediacy of the moment, you might see that the brushfire that is currently destroying many aspects of your life is clearing the path for new growth. A field that has been ravaged by fire can sprout new plants that may be stronger, healthier, and more diverse than those that previously existed, leading to a rich, sustainable ecosystem. It's hard to see in the charred wasteland that is the after-effect of a fire, but coming back a few short months later, you will witness a miracle of emerging new growth.

After a divorce, life continues in ways that prove this point. We all come to answers to many of our most distressing questions, such as, "How will I support myself financially?" The intensity of grief gradually fades. But there's a critical difference between simply surviving the process and truly flourishing. What creates the difference is the eye of the beholder.

Flowers after Fire

An Appreciative Eye

When people can see a growth-inducing positive in the present, they have an appreciative eye. Everyone has an appreciative eye sometimes, and when they are using it, they exhibit the following qualities:

- Persistence
- Conviction that one's actions matter
- Tolerance for uncertainty
- Irrepressible resilience

You can see how these qualities can lead to success following and during divorce. A tolerance for uncertainty – and there is a lot of uncertainty during divorce – coupled with the conviction that one's actions matter leads a person to make smart choices about behavior and to persist in them even when times get tough. Irrepressible resilience, the ability to bounce back higher from challenges than the original starting point, is a natural consequence of the other three qualities, and it also feeds back into them.

Here are four techniques suggested by Thatchenkerry and Metzker that I found invaluable during my divorce:

Tool 1: Change Your Stories

Fill your mind with success stories. Talk to people who have navigated divorce and are now thriving. Seek out stories of people who have achieved great things, even in the face of tremendous obstacles. Reframe your own negative stories as either closed chapters (if you are not still in the midst of their unfolding) or as necessary chapters in the eventual successful conclusion of your own book.

Tool 2: Change Your Reflections

Consciously choose the thoughts that fill your mind as you go through your day. Practice looking for new and positive possibilities in people and situations, and you will begin to see potential in your surroundings.

Tool 3: Change Your Questions

Find areas in your life where you are feeling strong and successful. Fill your mind with questions about those situations. What are the circumstances that help me feel strong here? What meaning am I finding in this situation? What's possible now?

Tool 4: Talk to Someone Different

We can easily become stuck in our own patterns of thought. By seeking the perspectives of those who are outside our situation, preferably those who themselves possess a mindset of growth and possibility, we open ourselves to new solutions and a wider view of reality.

What Brings a Sparkle to Your Eye?

With the eye trained for possibility, your life will be rich with meaning, and you will recognize creative ways to use the resources that are available to you to rise to new heights.

Discussion

Senia: This is not an application of positive psychology I expected, and your writing shows that positive psychology was pretty much made to deal with divorce in a productive way.

Maria: This is a really good article. I'll share it with a couple of my friends. I especially enjoyed the part that had the words, "With the eye trained for possibility…" To succeed one has to train the eye and learn from anything that happens to be in front of us.

Kristen M.: Your perspective certainly rings true to me. My parents divorced 10 years ago, when I was 19. I hit the ground running, and grew tremendously. I know that I would not have grown into the strong, compassionate, independent woman I am today had I not been forced to grow in the mud.

My parents have a warm, solid relationship now and we are still a family. My brothers have grown into responsible, contented go-getters who appreciate life as it unfolds. My parents' marriage ended; their relationship changed and healed, and our family transformed beautifully. It is possible to grow stronger, wiser, and happier from such an experience. I'm glad you remind people that there is hope during such a difficult and painful transition.

Kirsten: Thank you for sharing your experience. You are a great example of just the spirit of hope and strength that I want to bring to the world. My vision does not deny the pain that exists along the way, but it holds out the message that life does not stop there, especially if you have things in place, like good support networks. I appreciate your comment.

Chapter 10 In Praise of Praise by Timothy T. C. So

 *Timothy T. C. So is a Ph.D. candidate in Psychology in the Department of Psychiatry, University of Cambridge, a project coordinator and senior fellow of Harvard University's Institute of Coaching, and the President of the Global Chinese Positive Psychology Association.*

"The praise that comes from love does not make us vain, but more humble." J. M. Barrie, the author of *Peter Pan* (1860 – 1937)

Today is my graduation ceremony for my Masters degree, a big and significant day. This sweet and warm moment makes me think of what I learned about praise and appreciation from Professor Michael West, now the Executive Dean of Aston Business School.

My Personal Experience

I have to admit I was really lazy as a student, even when I was in college. When I made the decision to do my Masters abroad, I just set a simple goal to learn as much as I could so that I could catch up for my academically wasted time. However, as you can imagine, I was quite unconfident and always worried about my weak foundation in front of my bright fellow students. Yet I was blessed enough to be supervised by this great teacher who appreciated and encouraged me all the way through this year.

As an occupational psychologist, one of Michael's research interests is the importance of feedback in organizations. He knows how to appreciate everyone around him and is never stingy with sincere encouragement and praise. I remember when I shared with him my thoughts and plans in our first meeting. No matter how naive my ideas were, he listened attentively. He was always able to appreciate my efforts and find something desirable in my ideas. He was determined to keep me working hard on research and doing what is worth doing. Without all his appreciation, praise, and support, I would not have done so well in every paper I wrote.

Graduation Celebration

Michael praises, and he knows how to praise. He seldom praises people for who they are, but focuses on how much effort they exerted and how they approached a task. This type of praise tends to be more effective in motivating people to do better.

Everyone loves being praised and appreciated. Appreciation promotes positive emotion, more satisfying relationships, and improved coping with stress. Expressing appreciation to others also helps build social bonds.

Why Is Praise So Seldom Used?

Imagine that you are in a world without praise, appreciation, or encouragement: it would be like existing in complete darkness without light. No matter how hard you work, happiness would seem unreachable. It costs us so little to appreciate nice things around us, or to express praise to others. Yet we often take people for granted, and instead amplify trivial upsets.

It is particularly apparent in Asian societies. East Asians, especially the Japanese and Chinese, tend to be self-critical instead of self-enhancing. East Asian parents usually downplay their children's successes and highlight their children's failures whereas American parents do the opposite.

This story might happen in Asian families: a boy comes home in a good mood, and tells Mum that he got 90 out of 100 on his test. Mum asks him why he didn't get the full 100. Later the boy returns happily with the full 100 mark on another test, and his Mum says that academic results mean nothing, and that conduct is more important. The boy keeps working hard and behaving himself, and finally gets a conduct award. His Mum says disdainfully, "And so? Your school is actually not very good." This probably happens because of a positive intention – never praise your children or they will become too arrogant and not further improve. But you can imagine how disappointed and frustrated the child would be.

An Educational Perspective on Praise

Yes, it might be hard for parents who seldom praise their children to start complimenting them. Yet it can become easier to express compliments when we recall the joyful and fulfilled feelings that accompany receiving praise. Keep in mind that praise does not mean simply saying good things to your child or student. Praise should be specific and concrete so that children learn which behaviors are good and thus can perform them more frequently.

It can be detrimental to praise children for whatever they do without considering how they do it. Praising inherent characteristics (such as appearance) but not praising actual behavior may actually hinder future performance improvement. Praising effort regardless of quality may be detrimental as well. It is important to identify and praise the efforts that lead to effective performance and mastery of essential skills.

An Organizational Perspective on Praise

Praise and appreciation can also be used in organizations. A scientific study, which surveyed over 4 million employees worldwide from more than 10,000 business units and around 30 industries, found that individuals who receive regular recognition and praise have higher individual productivity and engagement compared to their colleagues. They are also more likely to stay with their organizations, and they receive higher customer scores on loyalty and satisfaction.

How much does it cost to achieve this? The techniques are actually almost free. They include recognizing an individuals' work, showing appreciation by cards or thank-you notes, finding out what others' real needs and complaints are and visibly responding to them, and giving praise.

When **Thomas Edison** was thrown out by his school, his mother's praise and appreciation reassured him. **Margaret Thatcher** believed that praise and encouragement from her father prompted her achievement. **Walt Disney** once said "You can dream, create, design and build the most wonderful place in the world. But it requires people to make that dream a reality." Yes, we can dream, create, design, and build the most wonderful place in the world, but it would not become reality if there were only criticism and no appreciation.

I would like to express my gratitude to everyone who gave me a hand during my studies. Every bit of encouragement, help, advice, and support played a significant role in my development. Thank you!

Special thanks to my beloved parents who never stopped their care and support even for one second. Your love has always reached me from thousands of miles away to the United Kingdom!

Note: *The article that turned into this chapter was written in 2007 when Timothy So obtained his Msc degree in Occupational Psychology.*

Discussion

Margaret: CONGRATULATIONS on your academic achievement! I love the way you took this opportunity to express your gratitude to your professor, parents, and others who helped you along the way. Your heartfelt appreciation and sincerity shine through.

Anonymous: I have learned so much from your article on the subject of praise and appreciation. I hope families will awaken from the great mistake of perpetually pointing out mistakes and failures, and not noticing little drops of successes in their children.

PART IV: GRATITUDE HOLIDAYS

Holidays are times to celebrate and to reinforce traditions that connect us to our pasts, our families, and our cultures. The chapters in this part suggest ways that we extend our traditional celebrations to increase gratitude and well-being.

In *Gratitude Day*, Derrick Carpenter concludes that his Thanksgiving traditions, in spite of being fun and pleasant, are in need of repair because they depart from the traditional meaning of the day. He starts a new tradition that causes him to reflect deeply on the things in the preceding year that evoke gratitude.

In *Reflections on Thanksgiving*, Angus Skinner compares the American Thanksgiving to the quieter harvest festivals of his native Scotland. After gathering in the harvest, people experience good will that prepares for winter. They also slow down to savor what is good in life. Then perhaps they can find the generosity of spirit that will change the world.

Like most of us, Gail Schneider has broken many resolutions made on New Years. In *An Appreciative New Years,* she ponders beginning the year by appreciating what is already working well rather than making resolutions to fix what she doesn't like about herself.

In *Mother's Day*, Giselle Nicholson reviews the history of this holiday. In the United States, it was originally a time for mothers to advocate for causes such as peace and healthy communities. She also reflects on making the occasion reinforce the things we value.

Chapter 11 Gratitude Day by Derrick Carpenter

 *Derrick Carpenter, MAPP '07, is a founder of Vive Training where he coaches individuals and corporate clients on creating high-engagement lifestyles through physical and psychological wellness.*

Holidays, such as Thanksgiving, are times for tradition. The idiosyncrasies that make up my family's holiday traditions are precisely the reasons I look forward to the holiday season all year. What would this fourth week in November be in America without turkey, football, and the Macy's Thanksgiving Day Parade? My personal Thanksgiving favorites include enjoying my mom's indulgent chocolate cream pie and our family game of Trivial Pursuit after dinner.

While most of the traditions in which I take part bring me closer to the important people in my life, it occurred to me recently that these traditions are gross misinterpretations of what this holiday was originally meant to celebrate.

Thanksgiving was first observed by European settlers in the Americas as both a harvest festival and a religious observance. In its earliest forms, it was often a day of fasting. When the holiday was celebrated with a feast—which only happened when the harvest was generous—the meal consisted of foods native to America that were new to the European settlers. Given the New England climate and the technology of the mid-17th century, these early Thanksgiving traditions were truly about giving thanks for things that couldn't be depended upon. We say grace before our meal, and I do feel grateful for the food, but it is quite a different kind of thanks knowing that grocery stores are open 24 hours throughout the holiday weekend. Something has been lacking from my holiday traditions. My Thanksgiving was in need of repair.

I turned to the character strength, Gratitude, for an answer. Thanksgiving is Gratitude Day! My Thanksgiving traditions, albeit cozy and harmless, were missing meaningful personal gratitude. So this year I set out to establish a new Gratitude Day tradition: to compile a list of one hundred things I am sincerely grateful for within the past year.

I had simple rules. Each item had to be something personal (I couldn't be grateful that puppies exist) and non-obvious (I couldn't be grateful for the air I breathe). I was quite intimidated at first and feared that I might have a difficult time. About a dozen or so came right out, things that I had been thinking about while conceiving of the idea, including a handful of poignant conversations with close friends and the gorgeous night sky I saw in Oregon earlier this fall. Then I felt stuck for a few minutes.

But once I got into a stride, points of gratitude came from every direction: the people I've met, the places I've been, the experiences from which I learned and grown! By the time I jotted down the hundredth thing, I sat back in amazement over how full this year has been.

A daily gratitude journal can be fulfilling, but looking back on much larger time scales—a year or a decade—can give a whole new perspective on life.

Looking Up into a Starry Sky

I intend to uphold the creation of this list as an annual tradition on Gratitude Day. Now that I am more aware of how fortunate I am, I feel better prepared to face the coming weeks of Christmas insanity with a clear head. I highly recommend this exercise for anyone seeking a way to reconnect with the deeper meanings and older traditions of the holiday season.

Discussion

Senia: I could imagine you getting more and more caught up in the details as you remembered the year. One hundred things every Thanksgiving! There's something wonderful about creating your own new tradition. Thanks for the idea.

Cathy H.: I like this. I started a tradition of sending "Happy Gratitude Day" e-cards a few years ago. I use my fall photography, so in a way I can savor fall colors while sharing gratitude with others. I also design my own Christmas Cards with a list of my 12 blessings for the year. Reading between the lines of the blessings, one gets a Christmas letter with a very positive focus. I say we change the name to Gratitude Day!!!

Dalida: It was interesting to read your article. I am not American, and Thanksgiving is not part of my upbringing. I am amazed how gratitude shifts my perspective. I started writing a Gratitude Journal a month ago and I am now totally addicted to the positive feelings that are generating a positive outlook, more creativity, and a proactive approach to life. Your idea of doing year/decade gratitude lists is another insight I gain. Thanks for sharing!

Saira: As some other readers have mentioned, I am not an American either, but I could totally relate to your observations about how many of us have something missing in our holidays, and how we can re-invent the completeness with a touch of personalization and gratitude. No doubt gratitude has been presented as the basis of contentment and satisfaction in a variety of religions. I find this truly insightful.

Chapter 12 Reflections on Thanksgiving by Angus Skinner

Angus Skinner, MAPP '06, works in his beloved and beautiful Scotland as a visiting Professor at the University of Strathclyde.

Europeans generally don't celebrate Thanksgiving. We have important, though quieter, harvest festivals, and we wish you North Americans ease in yours. The Thanksgiving celebration of harvest gathered in sits between Diwalli (Hindu) and Christmas (pagan in its timing). Celebrations matter in the rhythm of life.

Good will is the hallmark of autumnal and winter festivals across the world. We don't hibernate alone, as we might if we were bears. We huddle together for warmth, for comfort, and for joy.

Joy is much under-rated, an emotion that stands on its own, rather than depending on practical achievements. Christians will think of the Mary and Martha story, Mary who sat at the feet of Jesus while Martha prepared the meal. But all faiths have parallels. And all have both celebrations and the days after. Finding joy in the days after is the challenge of well-being.

Harvest Festival

Positive emotions were much underrated during the 20th century. But the world has changed. Fear, including fear of ourselves, is being addressed. It is good to celebrate the harvest of positive psychology, attained and growing.

Of course this harvest will barely provide for a year. We will have to work for the blessings of the year. Joseph's dream of the 7 fat cows followed by 7 lean cows partly alerts people to the dangers and partly provides a way forward.

Thanksgiving is, I guess, a time for family engagement (with all its embarrassments). The morning after is time for taking stock.

And in taking stock for the future, we can slow down, savor, enjoy, engage in life, build meaning and purpose, take risks for others, and be present with purpose. These seem better hallmarks than all the various me-centered goals.

Helping change the world takes generosity of spirit in action, of which there is more than enough to produce next year's harvest – if we do the work. If we do the work to let it grow, then it will flow. Next year beckons.

Discussion

Louise L.: Hello from California! A Google Search served up your wonderful post, and I just had to say thank you, not just because it's Thanksgiving over here but because I love 'connecting the dots' with people who encourage others to slow down and take stock of their lives.

Chapter 13 An Appreciative New Year by Gail Schneider

Gail A. Schneider, J.D., MAPP '07, brings to positive psychology an extensive background from the world of big business. After a 20 year career at JPMorgan Chase where she was an Executive Vice-President, she now works and writes on the issues of life transitions and the search for meaning and purpose in mid-life.

It's that time of year again. If you are Type A and goal-oriented like I am, your annual list of New Year's resolutions is beginning to take shape. My usual approach has been to look back on the year gone by and identify all the many things I wanted to accomplish and didn't, a sobering exercise at best and one guaranteed to put the "Bah, Humbug" mindset into holiday celebrations!

In prior years, I would construct my new resolutions on the shaky foundation of last year's failures. I didn't get to the gym enough last year. This next year, I'd typically resolve to go 5 days a week, maybe even 6. As a writer, I never did meet my goal of waking every morning and going straight to my computer for 3-4 uninterrupted hours of writing a day, so that makes another candidate for the top of the list. I think you get the picture.

As you might expect, somewhere around mid to late January, my motivation and enthusiasm for my new set of resolutions fell flatter than a day-old flute of champagne.

This year, I am determined to change and see what happens when I use an appreciative approach instead.

Fireworks for the New Year

Asking Appreciative Questions

My first step is to *inquire appreciatively* about what went right for me in the previous year. The idea of focusing on what has worked well rather than on what has not can be a powerful way to promote change.

For example, when I look back at when I was most successful last year in maintaining a consistent pattern of exercise, I notice that it was the several months right before the presidential election. I was riveted by the primary season and once the candidate slates were selected, they never failed to disappoint. Several days of the week I'd go to the gym and watch MSNBC and CNN simultaneously, switching between the 2 channels depending on the images on the screen and the crawl below. Before I knew it I had done 50 minutes on the elliptical machine without ever having looked at my watch.

Now I know I can't wait another *four* years before I go back to the gym, and even *I* have a limit for listening to pundits speculating about the Obama's search for a new puppy, but I have learned that exercising while engaged in watching something that captures my attention makes the time fly by.

Recognizing and Being Grateful for My Wins

Finally I plan to add the practice of gratitude to the New Year's resolution process. Each of us may not have the self-regulation required to keep a nightly gratitude journal, but this time of year is a natural point of endings and beginnings, and so it is a perfect time for introspection and reflection on the many reasons we have to be grateful. It is through the lens of gratitude that I choose to look forward to the next year and on that far sturdier foundation that I plan my future.

A Small Gift to You

In closing, I have a small gift. It is one of my favorite poems. It is taped to the inside of a closet door in my home office.

While I wish every reader a year of good health and happiness, this is a gift for when life disappoints, and you face challenges, even those that blindside you and take your breath away. I have been there and this poem has comforted me.

The Guest House
By Rumi
Translated by Coleman Barks in *The Essential Rumi*

This being human is a guest house.
Every morning a new arrival.

A joy, a depression, a meanness,
Some momentary awareness comes
as an unexpected visitor.

Welcome and entertain them all!
Even if they're a crowd of sorrows,
who violently sweep your house
empty of its furniture,
still, treat each guest honorably.
He may be clearing you out
for some new delight.

The dark thought, the shame, the malice,
meet them at the door laughing,
and invite them in.

Be grateful for whoever comes,
because each has been sent
as a guide from beyond.

Discussion

Wayne: The irony is that the yoga class is actually working on your self-regulation chip. One of the themes that underlies yoga is the development of mindfulness – awareness of thinking but without judgment.

And interestingly as you become more mindful, goals (New Year's resolutions) become less important.

Good luck in discovering your inner wisdom.

Senia: Thanks for throwing in the wonderful poem by Rumi! I am going to pin that one up as well.

Kirsten: Thank you so much, Gail, for this article, and especially for the poem by Rumi. I don't feel at all like that's a small gift at the end of your article – I feel like it's the most powerful part. Rumi's suggestion (so beautifully phrased) that we drink in all of life's experiences – the pleasant, the humbling, the ecstatic, the devastating – each as valuable as the others, is at the heart of true growth and authenticity and love. I think it's through this very act (which is sometimes called mindfulness or nonattachment) that we become powerfully courageous to tackle the world in ways that are far beyond any goal list we would normally come up with.

Louis: Thanks for this article, Gail. I've been thinking about New Year's goals for the past few days, and this certainly helps me frame the possibility of an abundant year. I wish the same for you.

Gail: The common thread that runs through this discussion is the importance of being present to your life, accepting what it brings and trying to find the message and the meaning in it, even in the dark times.

For the poetry lovers, another great one with a similar theme is *Love after Love* by Derek Walcott.

Chapter 14 Mother's Day by Giselle Nicholson

Giselle Nicholson, MAPP '06, is an aspiring social entrepreneur. Giselle is a Senior Analyst for Blue Garnet Associates. She also facilitates leadership development and team-building seminars based on positive psychology in Southern California.

Humans gravitate towards creating and celebrating rituals in all sizes and forms – from a morning shower routine to the composition of an elaborate Thanksgiving dinner. Rituals are a way for us to recognize our values and connect to what creates meaning for us. Many believe that rituals give us a rhythm to stabilize our stressful and chaotic lives. By engaging in ritualistic behavior we are able to ground ourselves and reconnect to others. When rituals become commonly observed, sometimes we make holidays of them. However, Mother's Day in the United States, a holiday to recognize the value of mothers, started without established rituals.

Despite rumors or cynicism, Mother's Day is not a holiday that was created by Hallmark. However, it has evolved in such a way that perhaps the cynics have a point. Celebrations for mothers date back to the annual spring festival the Greeks dedicated to Rhea, the mother of many deities, and to the offerings ancient Romans made to their Great Mother of Gods, Cybele. Christians celebrated this festival on the fourth Sunday in Lent in honor of Mary, mother of Christ. In England this holiday was expanded to include all mothers and was called Mothering Sunday.

Mother's Day Tray

Where Did Mother's Day Come From?

Mother's Day in the United States dates back about 150 years. An Appalachian mother, Anne Jarvis, organized a day to raise awareness of poor health conditions in her community, a cause she believed would be best advocated by mothers. She called it "Mother's Work Day." Fifteen years later, Julia Ward Howe, a Boston poet, pacifist, and suffragist had similar ideals after the Civil War when she attempted to create a formal Mother's Day for Peace. She believed mothers bore the loss of human life more harshly than anyone else.

When Anne Jarvis died, her daughter Anna began to lobby businessmen and politicians to create a special day to honor mothers. The first such Mother's Day was celebrated in Grafton, West Virginia, on May 10, 1908, in the church where Anne Jarvis had taught Sunday school. Five years later, the House of Representatives adopted a resolution calling for officials of the federal government to wear white carnations on Mother's Day. In 1914, Woodrow Wilson signed a bill recognizing Mother's Day as a national holiday.

From Gratitude Letters and Church to Dining Out and the Highest Phone Traffic

At first, people observed Mother's Day by attending church, writing letters to their mothers (gratitude letters!), and eventually, by sending cards, presents, and flowers. As the commercialization of Mother's Day increased, Jarvis became more and more enraged and became an opponent of what the holiday had become. She believed that the day's sentiment was being sacrificed for greed and profit. So in 1923 she filed a lawsuit to stop a Mother's Day festival, and was even arrested for disturbing the peace at a convention selling carnations for a war mother's group. Before her death in 1948, Jarvis is said to have confessed that she regretted ever starting the mother's day tradition.

Mother's Day is one of the most commercially successful holidays in the United States - the most popular day of the year to dine out and the day telephone companies record their highest traffic. Although I don't believe that flowers, lovely dinners, and pampering are bad ways to celebrate our mothers, I do think it's important that we understand the meaning behind our rituals. I don't know a single mother who doesn't treasure her homemade gifts most. I think there are some ways that we can be more cognizant about how we display our values through a holiday. By doing away with bells and whistles, we can focus on what matters most within our family so that we can find our lives filled with meaning and happiness.

From my observations, the most treasured family rituals are usually interesting, fulfilling, and fun. They typically involve family, friends, faith, nature, charity, giving, music, the arts, and food. The gratitude letter is most appropriate for today and best honors Mother's Day history.

I think it's also important to remember that in the United States, this holiday started as a way for mothers to advocate for causes, namely healthy communities and peace. Let's not forget that this is a day to celebrate the milestones of all women and the positive influence and impact that mothers have in making our world better. By knowing more about the history of this day we can be more aware of the meaning behind our actions and how our holiday rituals reinforce what we value.

All that being said, turn off your computer and go make your mother feel fantastic on Mother's Day!

Discussion

Senia: I never knew the history! It sounds like it was more a work day at first rather than the relaxing day it is now.

Angus: Thank you Giselle, this is history I did not know. My lovely mother died many years ago but she would have loved to read your account, as did I. I think you are absolutely right to emphasize the importance of rituals, ceremonies, and events, along with their value and meaning.

I am in awe really of all that my mother achieved, loving the five of us children, herself the youngest of eight and pretty much in control of her 7 brothers. She built the first primary school in Jallalpur Jattan (Pakistan) where I was born. My mum was born in Bornesketaig, Skye in a two roomed 'black house' that housed animals as well as the family and she was the first girl from there to go to University. As a missionary, she carried her religious views lightly as well as practically. As I reflect she was always close to delight and happy to engage with people of all faiths in that delight. We seem to be losing her innocence of perception, and I am fearful of the consequences. Your piece reminded me of the importance of my mother in my values and basic compass. Thank you.

Giselle: Angus, Thank you for sharing your mother's extraordinary achievements. From your orange socks to your quick smiles and laughter I can see that you share in your mother's delight for life.

You bring up such an important concept about birthdays, Mother's Day, Father's Day, and even anniversaries.

Our rituals celebrate our values, and these special days are really about cherishing the values that we share with our families and loved ones. They shape who we are and how we touch others.

PART V: GIFTS AND GRATITUDE

Part V explores the interplay between gifts and gratitude.

In *An Abundant Season*, Louis Alloro suggests ways to invent new rituals for celebrating holidays with family and friends, rituals that involve gifts of dialogue, gratitude, and time. These rituals do not have to be brand new. He contemplates updating a ritual from his childhood for recognizing good deeds.

Sometimes people run out of ideas for holiday gifts or want to give something different, particularly for people who already have too many things. In *Happiness Gifts*, Kathryn Britton lists more than 20 kinds of gifts that contribute to happiness in different ways.

In *Thank You Notes*, Aren Cohen discusses how she made writing thank you notes for wedding gifts a joyful opportunity to connect with her friends rather than a chore.

If pure altruism is doing something good for someone else without receiving any benefit, does it exist in the world? In *The Gift of Giving*, Derrick Carpenter argues that the lack of pure altruism is a truly beautiful thing because it stems from an innate human disposition to enjoy helping others.

Chapter 15 An Abundant Season by Louis Alloro

 *Louis Alloro, M.Ed., MAPP '08, works with individuals, organizations, and communities as a change agent -- coaching, training, and facilitating towards positive growth affecting people, planet, and profit. www.LouisAlloro.com*

With the advent of the holiday season, many of us prepare to celebrate Christmas, Hanukkah, and Kwanzaa—holidays that traditionally involve giving gifts to people we love.

But many of us are strapped for cash. That stress sits on top of the stress about finding the perfect gifts. What if we consider alternative ways this year to show the ones we love that we love them? That's what it's all about, anyway, right?

Let's make the next holiday season a creative challenge: an opportunity to invent new rituals for being with family and friends.

Gifts of Dialogue

It is important to think about our underlying belief systems that hold these gift-giving traditions alive. Conversations about strengths and values can strengthen connections.

Talking about strengths can spark such discussion: what strengths do we most call on when giving gifts?

Some questions we might ask are:

- Why do we give gifts?
- What do they symbolize?
- What do we, as a family, symbolize?
- What do we value as a group?
- How can we take what we value and create customs and traditions that line up with those values?
- How can we open ourselves to ideas from traditions other than our own?

Gifts of Gratitude

We can give gratitude as a gift. Writing a gratitude letter requires that we tap into our hearts to find words that show our love for another person or words that express the strength we see in someone else.

Not a good letter writer? How about writing a poem? Many of the ones we read in high school, you could have written too. Remember, short lines, and they don't have to rhyme. It's about communicating how you feel.

You could also create an artistic collage, a compact disk, or playlist to give to your loved ones.

With whatever medium, the way this gift comes alive is in how it is presented. Reading the letter aloud to the recipient or listening to the playlist together gives both the giver and receiver moments to be thankful for.

Gifts of Time

We can also give the gift of time. Our common bonds are strengthened by spending time as a family and experiencing positive emotions together. Playing games can build collective efficacy and hope. Singing and dancing together have many benefits. Anyone up for caroling?

Perhaps you and your family can give your collective time for a worthy cause. There are plenty of opportunities in your own back yard. Friends of mine have been calling bingo at a senior center and leave each week rejuvenated and even elated.

Thinking Outside the Box

I remember fondly from my childhood creating a manger for baby Jesus in preparation for Christmas. My mom cut yellow strips of construction paper and laid them next to an empty basket. Each time we did a good deed during the Christmas season, we wrote it on a strip and laid it in the basket.

Come Christmas Eve, the basket was full of "hay" and we would read all of the intentional good things we had done in the past month to "pay it forward." I'll never forget that experience.

Good Deed Basket

Maybe I'll suggest that my family do that again this year. Of course, it will be more challenging since we're all grown up and live separately from one another. But I'm sure we can create a virtual manger online somewhere to make this possible. It's time to think outside the box.

Being a Gracious Host

We can ***invite our families and friends into an abundant and stress-free holiday season***. Find the people in your spheres of influence that see the value in this opportunity and get them on board right away. How can we use this seemingly bad economic time to find ways to contribute to our well-being – ways that spending money can never truly show anyhow?

Discussion

Nadya: Thank you, Louis, for reminding us of creative and meaningful ways to show love and appreciation this holiday season! The economic crisis is in fact a blessing in disguise in that it shifts our attention to the deep well of kindness and generosity that we find within and that only grows deeper as our ability to find distraction in consumption diminishes.

Jeremy: I always find the holidays a time to consider the meaning in our lives. Your article gives some great foundations for having a dialogue with those closest to us.

Vickie: I especially love the gratitude letter idea. And the gift of time is so meaningful. Wouldn't it be wonderful if we gave our kids our time instead of hiring a babysitter while we shop for them?

Wayne: How about learning to give to yourself?

Louis: I do think that learning to savor and be mindful is important. How can you turn that individual solo lesson into something you bring to those you love and suggest they incorporate those practices into their lives?

Wayne: It's called emotional contagion.

Louis: Yes! I totally believe in the power of emotional contagion, but I'm wondering, how do you think we can make this more intentional? How can we give these ideas as gifts this holiday season?

Wayne: The gift is simple – manage your own emotion and it impacts other people. No rocket science here.

Margaret: Here are 2 more ideas from our family:

1. Bake cookies together and then give them away to friends, family, shelters, neighbors, and so on. My college-aged daughter just wrote a paper for her English Folklore class on what this tradition has meant to her.

2. Collect your favorite photos from years past and create individualized 2009 calendars to give to family and friends.

Caryn: Who'da thunk the idea of my most precious resource, time with you, could also be used as a Christmas gift! It does amaze me why I have so little time for myself because I always want to give it away! As I bought myself a vacuum for Christmas, I will also buy myself time alone, for mindfulness, prayer and correction of direction (only if needed). As Joyce Meyer said, sometimes, we are only to be seeing, doing, etc. for one season, not all seasons.

Chapter 16 Happiness Gifts by Kathryn Britton

 *Kathryn Britton, MAPP '06, is a coach, adjunct instructor at the University of Maryland, and associate editor of Positive Psychology News Daily. She works toward positive workplaces where people can be highly productive and satisfied with work that they find meaningful.*

For many cultures, the end of the year is a time to give gifts. Have you ever wondered how to select gifts that have an ongoing positive impact? Do you have people on your list who say "No more stuff, please?" Are there others who are hard to please? Have you been giving gifts to someone for so long that it is hard to think of anything?

Get new ideas from the three pathways to happiness: The Pleasant Life, The Engaged Life, and The Meaningful Life.

For the Pleasant Life: Remember that people are different when it comes to savoring pleasant things. Some get more pleasure out of remembering things that have already happened, others are more in the moment, and others get more out of anticipating things that haven't happened yet. You might reflect on which kind of pleasure is strongest for the person you are thinking about.

For pleasure in anticipation:

- Give tickets to a concert or play. Maybe buy yourself a ticket and go along for the shared experience.
- Promise a distant friend or relative a visit later in the year.
- Give a promise for a rarely enjoyed pleasure such as dinner in a topnotch restaurant.
- Give a child a treasure chest of coupons redeemable for activities with you. For example, give coupons for a card game or a trip to a ball game or even 24 hours of your time to be used all at once or spread over the next year.

For pleasure in the moment:

- Give gifts that require attention to sensory input. I remember a wine tasting kit that helped us pinpoint different aspects of taste.
- Collect feedback on the gifts you give and use that to help the person explore a range of tastes. My husband gives me chocolate and asks for my opinions of each variety. Over time, he has built up an extensive picture of what I like.

For pleasure in remembering:

- Construct a scrapbook with pictures and objects that remind the receiver of a trip or special occasion.
- Make a calendar with pictures that capture the family history of the prior year.
- Create a book or poster of family genealogy along with pictures and family stories.
- Record concerts or performances given by members of the family and give the recordings.

- Some people have great stories from long and full lives but are not interested in writing. Give the services of a personal biographer to interview and do the writing. (I learned this one from Margaret.)

For the Engaged Life, give gifts that grow skills, that are challenging but not impossibly so, that give frequent feedback, and that the receiver believes are intrinsically worth doing. Helping somebody explore something new is a gift in itself.

- Encourage nature-watching habits. For example, give bird feeders, bluebird houses, or binoculars. Such supplies can often convert a passive interest into an active one.

Watching a Bird Feeder

- Give dance lessons or music lessons. Maybe you could take the lessons together.
- Give materials and lessons for arts and handcrafts. I remember the pleasure of receiving a brand-new paint box with a wide assortment of colors.
- Give books that challenge and uplift. This is particularly important for adolescents, who are often assigned very grim and discouraging books at school.
- Give scrapbooking materials and help someone work through photographs to represent a personal history.

For the Meaningful Life, give gifts that help others live in service of something larger than themselves, whether that be the family or the local community or the world at large.

- Give cooking lessons that include preparing food for the local soup kitchen. For example, teach your children to roast a turkey, and then take it together.
- Set up a monthly conference call for your widely dispersed family so you tell and listen to each other's stories.
- Give someone a trip to visit someone else that they love but have not seen for years.
- Give a gift to a charity of your friend's choice in his or her honor. It is always fun to give bees or parts of water buffaloes through the Heifer Project. My local friends do this at Christmas, but we always ask to find out the charity of choice this year.
- Give someone your time working together on a local volunteer project of their choice. Perhaps it will mean going together to the soup kitchen once a month or working together on a Habitat for Humanity project or at the hospital or wherever is close to your friend's heart.

These are just a few ideas to prime your thinking about gifts that give pleasure through memory, experience, or anticipation, that absorb attention, or that help people live in service of something larger than themselves.

Discussion

Jeff: I like the idea of buying non-goods type gifts, creating fun, and important experiences, like Adopting a Whale or whatnot. Awesome!

Senia: I love it that your husband knows more about your taste in chocolates with each continuing year. There's something quite magical about that.

Chapter 17 Thank You Notes by Aren Cohen

 *Aren Cohen, MAPP '07, MBA, is formerly the Vice President of Business Development at FundingPost. She is now a learning coach for students in New York City. Her MAPP capstone research on the positive psychology of fathers and daughters used data from the Harvard Grant Study of Adult Development.*

Recently married, I have had cause to write numerous thank you notes. We know that Miss Manners insists that we write thank you notes, but aside from common courtesy, what are the benefits of writing them?

A visit to the Emily Post Institute website offers practical advice, "Schedule a few different days to write your notes, and each time give yourself a little something to make it interesting: music, a glass of wine, your favorite radio show, a cup of tea—perhaps even some chocolate." Yet these goodies don't reflect why writing thank you notes is good for the soul.

I recently saw a family friend whom I had thanked for a lovely gift. I was surprised that she said, "Your thank you note was so beautiful. Another friend also sent me a thank you note for a wedding present and it was so **nowhere**. I really appreciate you taking time to write something so thoughtful." I don't tell this story to blow my own horn, but I was curious about why my note was different. Perhaps it is my experience with positive psychology. A thank you note is a mini-dose of a gratitude letter or journal. It is an opportunity to flex your gratitude strength—one of the strengths of transcendence.

Writing a thank you note is a chance to acknowledge the other person and to thank them for thinking about you. They may have sent you something you will never use, but the fact that they thought about you is the significant act, and it is your job to acknowledge with genuine sincerity the kindness of their gesture. When you write a thank you note, you recognize that another person considered you, and in turn you exercise an opportunity to reciprocate by appreciating them.

Emily Post suggests that you find something to savor when you write your thank you notes. My personal favorite is beautiful stationary that I feel reflects my personality and taste.

More important than private savoring, when you write a thank you note, you get a chance to show the gift-givers that you are savoring the gifts they gave you and the fact that they took the time to think of you. Sharing your experience of savoring shows mindfulness and allows the gift-giver to share in pleasure you may get from the gift.

Finally, back to Miss Manners. We all know that the following thank you note just doesn't cut it.

Dear So-and-so,
Thank you so much for the present. It was so nice of you.
Warmly,
Me

A good thank you note is sincere and thoughtful. Get creative. The Emily Post website is correct that the process of writing a thank you note **should be a joy, not a chore**. Remember to tell the gift-givers that you are thankful not only for the gift, but also for their thinking of you. Tell them how you are looking forward to experiencing the gift.

Elegant Stationary to Savor

Even if you don't love the gift, there are other ways to let them know you appreciate the thought. In these tough economic times, acknowledge their generosity. Let them know that you look forward to seeing them again soon. Mind them, make them feel important and loved. In giving you the gift, they made you feel special.

You can, and should, return the favor.

Discussion

Marcial: Not to mention, Aren, that grateful people are the ones whose sleep patterns are the most relaxing and restoring.

When you are beginning to feel tired, close to sleep, in those few moments when you are in and out, it is a good moment to go to your heart, and think of a few ways you might be grateful that day. If you are one of those that have trouble going to sleep, it is going to take a few attempts. Easy and deep sleep will be the sign that gratefulness now resides in your heart.

Hans: The Christmas holidays are always a great time to think about the multitude of things we are grateful for and express it to the people we care about. I find a thoughtful note, a sincere gesture, or a warm hug can bring a precious moment. They remind me every time that caring and being cared about provide the fuel for living a happier and more fulfilling life each and every single day. Thank you Aren, your article is a nice reminder of this powerful but simple truth and the beauty of it is that the possibilities are endless.

Laura: "I saw this and thought of you..." is one of the most powerful tips given to me on teacher training. It can completely change a relationship with a challenging pupil if you can use this phrase. Taking an article out of a magazine on something they are interested in can spark new conversations; or even just saying that a character on television reminded you of them (and then explaining why) can be enough to make students realize that you think about them. It only costs time, but really does seem to make a difference. Great point!

Kathryn: Somehow this reminds me of grading papers — another activity that people often classify as a chore. I can see why. They've been piling up lately and seem like a mountain of work to get through. But when I am on a roll, I think of each one as an opportunity to say, "I see you!" to somebody.

I think we all crave moments when someone else says with word or deed, "I see you!" I also think it gets easier with practice — and more rewarding as well. Thanks for turning wedding gift thank-you notes into such an interesting reflection on saying thank you.

Aren: Kathryn, I think you might be right that the flip side to writing thank you notes is grading papers. Like writing thank you notes, the comments a teacher writes on a paper have an impact. People in general and students in particular need encouragement to learn and grow. A good teacher is a master at giving that kind of positive feedback.

As a tutor, I often see how teachers respond to students' papers, and what effect their words can have. Currently I have a pupil who has a very mean teacher. What hurts both me and my student the most is that this teacher does not acknowledge that the kid is TRYING HER BEST. Sometimes as teachers we get so caught up in our own expectations of what a student "should" be able to do, that we can't see those who might not meet our mark but are really putting forth their best efforts. Mindfulness means that we MUST lovingly encourage students to feel confident to continue trying to learn. Even a C-paper can get a note of encouragement if you tell a student what part of their essay you did respect, and how they can make it better.

Chapter 18 The Gift of Giving by Derrick Carpenter

 *Derrick Carpenter, MAPP '07, is a founder of Vive Training where he coaches individuals and corporate clients on creating high-engagement lifestyles through physical and psychological wellness.*

A few weeks back, I overheard a friend bemoan the lack of pure altruism in the world. **Pure altruism** is the act of doing something good to increase another person's well-being for which the giver receives no benefit. Let's give the search for pure altruism a closer look.

Theorists have used a divide-and-conquer approach to understand the foundations for altruism. Some of the biggest altruistic moves we make are for our children. Under a model of evolution in which individuals are invested in the survival of their genes, helping a relative – who shares some of your own genes – will accomplish this, so **altruism towards relatives** makes sense.

But we often do good deeds for friends and acquaintances as well. Some of these deeds are explained by the notion of **reciprocal altruism.** I will do a good deed for you now knowing that when I need help, you will return the favor. It's a sort of a social insurance policy.

But how can we account for the altruistic things we do without expectation of return, or, for that matter, the help we offer to complete strangers including people across the world that we will never see?

Is There Pure Altruism?

A recent study at the University of Oregon used functional MRI machines to observe changes in brain patterns of participants in different giving conditions. Participants were given $100, and some were given the option to donate a portion of the money to a charity while others were levied a mandatory tax that was given to the charity. For the subjects in the optional giving condition, the researchers attempted to remove any standard rewards for giving to charity, like enjoying the "warm glow" effect of others admiring your charitable deeds or avoiding the social shame of not giving. The subjects made their choices in privacy, without anyone else knowing how much, if any, money was donated. Many participants still donated. Was this pure altruism?

Even if the research participants received no public benefits and faced no public coercion to donate, that does not mean that they received no benefits. Perhaps doing a seemingly selfless deed simply gives us pleasure, a sense that we are meaningfully contributing to the world and making a difference. Psychological benefits are as good as any others.

Why are people so intent on unveiling an act of pure, selfless altruism? Such kindness would be accompanied by real pain and sacrifice, without any benefits, psychological or otherwise to the giver. I cannot understand why this type of giving is something of which we should be proud, if it does exist.

Humans get so caught up thinking about human inabilities that we take human abilities for granted. Car accidents reported on the evening news cause us to question what could have gone wrong. We much less frequently consider that millions of drivers successfully and safely navigate roadways at lethal speeds coming just a few feet from unforgiving obstacles every day. This is a truly remarkable and amazing human ability. Rather than groaning about the lack of pure altruism, perhaps we need to celebrate the grand human experience of feeling good when we commit an altruistic act. Our recipient benefits, but so do we. This seems part of the magic of the human experience.

Experiencing the Benefits of Altruism

On a whim, I decided to volunteer at the Philadelphia Marathon in mid-November hoping to be inspired to begin training myself. Since I was late to sign up, I was assigned to the race's bag check group, where runners could drop off personal items like wallets and clothing right before the race to be kept in a series of empty school buses and picked up as soon as they finished. This also meant I had to report to duty at 4:30am on Sunday. I braved the darkness and below-freezing weather with an unconvincing grin, waiting to view some feats of human achievement as runners finish the 26.2 mile trek.

As it turned out, the bag check station was completely closed off from the race, and we could see nothing. Dismayed, I worked with my fellow volunteers to organize bags for the runners assigned to our bus. The race began, and within a few hours, runners were pouring back in to retrieve their things. We handed back everything to our runners as fast as we could, knowing that they were freezing and desperate for their sweatpants and jackets.

Helping a Shivering Runner

The bus next to us, however, had had trouble organizing their bags, and a frustrated mob of cold runners was forming behind it. Watching them shiver in their shorts, I went over to help. I asked one or two dour-faced marathoners for their bib numbers and hopped on the bus to track them down. I was only able to help seven or eight runners, but the grateful looks on their faces when I returned their precious bags gave me a serious warm glow. While helping to relieve the tired and cold brave bodies of these runners, I completely forgot about how tired and cold I was.

The lack of pure altruism among humans is a truly beautiful thing, a consequence of our innate predispositions to help our fellow neighbor. Would any of us prefer to live in a world in which good deeds required pain and suffering? The seemingly paradoxical connection of selflessness and selfishness makes me smile with a sense of hope about the human condition. As you give gifts, I encourage you to be extra mindful of the happiness you experience as a result.

Discussion

Senia: I love the idea that something combining both selfishness and selflessness can be important. Your call to be mindful of one's own happiness is really delightful!

Christine: I agree with you in questioning the search for "pure" altruism — and love the fact that you question the idea that being kind is better if someone suffers to offer the kindness. Yes, it is wonderful to receive a kindness from someone else– it creates a lovely human connection– but to paraphrase what's been said for millennia, it often feels better when we give than when we receive. Isn't that a good thing?

Mark M.: Thanks Derrick, I caught an inspiring story on the news last night about The Kindness Offensive, 3 young guys who practice 'random acts of kindness and senseless acts of beauty.' That included handing out 25 tons of free food to the hungry and homeless.

Shirley: I love your point about selfless giving. To me, giving is always selfless because we cannot force anyone to do what we want. We can only give with good intentions and hope that it will be reciprocated.

Also as you stated, the happiness that results from giving, that warm feeling we experience, is the reason so many of us continue to give over and over again. Without the warm feeling, and the giving that comes from it, our world would be a bleaker place.

Jen: I don't know whether I feel better when I do something for someone on the sly, taking no credit for my deed, or when I'm praised for my effort. I suppose it depends upon how much time and energy I've dedicated to the project at hand. I do know that I get incredible personal satisfaction from some of the simplest deeds. Yep. Warm fuzzies, altruism, psychological stimulus – call it what you will. Doing good feels good.

PART VI: GRATITUDE IN THE FAMILY

Part VI celebrates that gratitude starts in the family.

In *Memories for a Grateful Future*, John Yeager describes his father's 80th birthday party where John's father-son competition and old memories of "not being a good enough son" were pushed aside by memories of being supported and reassured in a challenging moment.

In *From Vulnerability to Joy*, Sherri Fisher gives her recipe for moving from the vulnerability of the wedding to the joy of many years of shared marriage. Gratitude and appreciation are crucial ingredients.

Chapter 19 Memories for a Grateful Future by John Yeager

 *John M. Yeager, Ed.D, MAPP '06, is Director of the Center for Character Excellence at The Culver Academies in Culver, Indiana. As part of the Flourishing Schools group, John integrates best practices in education with positive psychology research.*

Sharing good news out loud with friends and family tends to increase the positive emotions and the sense of belonging. The more that positive emotions are shared, the greater likelihood that they will be remembered. People hearing about someone else's good fortune can make a big difference by responding with interest and enthusiasm. I know this from my positive psychology studies, so I decided to try it out at a recent family affair.

In early August, our family flew to Boston to attend a family reunion that also coincided with my father's 80th birthday. Prior to the trip, a variety of past images of "not being a good-enough son" permeated my brain. This included several real and some standard self-inflicted adversities that have wasted my emotional energy since childhood. I consciously decided that the reunion and birthday would be a celebration of my father's life, for all the good in him. I decided to make the event about him, not about me. This decision helped me to respond enthusiastically to his words and actions, to express gratitude for his being a good father, and to savor being with him during the reunion party.

By focusing on Dad and others, I was able recapture wonderful memories from childhood as I played badminton with my ten-year-old daughter. At one point, I called her by my sister's name – my sister looked similar at that age. I was back in time, and I basked in the warmth of sharing my positive childhood experiences with my daughter. When my father came into the game, I marveled at the athletic skills of a man in his ninth decade – instead of feeling competitive.

Family Badminton

This wasn't about living up to expectations. It was all about the good, and when my father spoke to the entire family about his orchestration of the event — he and my stepmother planned everything — there was not a dry eye. He explained that the party and reunion were about us, not him. It was about keeping the family connected. He did this for us.

After he spoke, an amazing calmness came over me. I asked for everyone's attention as I publicly spoke to Dad, reminding him of a time when I was 11 years old, and was fidgeting fearfully at the starting line of a 3-mile 4th of July road race. I realized that all the other runners were between 16 and 40 years of age. I was totally out of my league. I looked up at my father, and he appreciatively nodded his head and softly said to me, "It's okay. It will be fine." And it was, and still is!

This brief discussion is not about sharing my childhood issues of disappointment and competition. By changing my focus and showing gratitude, I had a powerful and fulfilling experience. I think I grew a lot that day as I made the lyrics of the Carly Simon song, *The Stuff that Dreams are Made Of,* come alive in my life:

> "Take a look around now
> Change the direction
> Adjust the tuning
> Try a new translation"

Discussion

Elona: What you have said is so true. When you change how you react to your environment, the environment changes the way it reacts to you. If you catch people being good, good catches you. Thanks for sharing your experience.

John: I love your feedback on the reciprocity of "catching people doing good." I will use this as a mantra for future events. Thanks.

Kathryn: This is a gift to those of us who know our parents won't be with us forever. It's a reminder that we have a choice about what we think about. It's also a reminder that no particular point in time defines an entire relationship and things go on changing all the way along.

I've been reading my grandfather's letters to my grandmother, written while he was an officer in France during World War I. His first son was born while he was away, so there are a lot of dreams and greetings to his baby at home. I happen to know that the reunion did not go well. Like many babies who meet their fathers long after birth, my uncle had trouble accepting his father, and my grandfather experienced great disappointment that his daydreams on the front didn't materialize the way he wanted.

I also know that my uncle was always there for both my grandparents up until the end. They called on him if they needed any help.

So either snapshot would be an incomplete representation of what was a relationship of many colors.

Thanks for your story, and Bravo!

David: Happy Birthday to your father, John! It's clear that you helped make his experience a positive one. And in so doing, you made everyone else's experience better too.

Chapter 20 From Vulnerability to Joy by Sherri Fisher

 *Sherri Fisher, MAPP '06, M.Ed., combines 25 years experience in PK-12 education with positive psychology to uncover engaged learning and working solutions for both individuals and organizations.*

To get along better with someone, do you have to be able to dance cheek-to-cheek? Maybe not, since being able to take risks and wing it together is a better predictor of marriage success than carefully choreographed steps. In honor of June, the wedding month in America, let's explore some aspects of human emotion that make for a joyful relationship.

Of course there are emotional risks when falling in love. To build a relationship with someone else involves some big risks. There's plenty you can do to appreciate what's good and working in a relationship and to get past "once bitten, twice shy" to broadening and building your connection.

Practice Gratitude

First of all, practice gratitude. You'll know that you are experiencing gratitude when you acknowledge that goodness exists, find that you have been the recipient of goodness from a source outside of yourself, and that as a result you feel happier and motivated to share and do good things yourself.

What are the benefits of gratitude to a relationship? One is the feeling of expanding from your self-oriented viewpoint and developing a future-versus-now way of thinking, something that is required even to get to the second date! Practicing gratitude also increases tolerance (something no relationship can do without), compassion, creativity, and, understanding for those moments where the other person's behavior is just plain confounding. The grateful exchange of intangible benefits leads to an upward spiral of love, bonding, empathy, wonder, and joy.

I Do! I Will!

Gratitude is not without challenges. Are things in the relationship running smoothly? You'll be giving yourself a pat on the back, since you know you are responsible. Are things not so good? You know it's not your fault, so what has your partner been doing wrong? Has your partner been especially loving and giving? You might struggle to feel gratitude if you think you don't deserve the goodness or think you deserve more.

Take an Appreciative View

Take an appreciative view of the other person. Even when something is not going well, lots of other things are. What are your partner's strengths? If you are feeling irritated, are you wearing your buttons out where they can be easily pushed? Perhaps your partner is your opposite, a wild and spontaneous person and you are self-regulated and making plans.

Try test-driving the other person's spontaneity strength. Split the difference: It's ok to set a time when you can just see what happens next. Be grateful when the unexpected comes along to sweep you off your feet.

Savor

Savor what's wonderful as a way to draw you closer. Stories matter. Listen to your wedding music together, show the wedding or honeymoon album to friends while you share remembrances of the big events. If you like to write, send letters to one another to savor the experience of beginning your life together. Are you drawn to beauty and excellence? Marvel together at a magnificent sunset or work of art. Let your senses luxuriate in a massage or a dinner out and share the story to savor it. Even practice anticipatory savoring while you plan a vacation or imagine a new home together.

Guard against Disgust

Frequent expression of disgust predicts relationship failure. When something disgusts you, what do you do? Think of a food which you really hate or the smell of something rotten. The overwhelming desire to spit something out can also be active in relationships. When someone else disgusts you, it is extremely difficult to like them. When you begin to feel disgust, switch to something—anything—admirable about the person. Everyone has something.

Talk about Good Things

Share good news with each other. Be enthusiastically interested in your partner's good news, even if you have to fake it until you make it. Be curious and listen for places to ask questions so that there is some give and take. An enthusiastic response makes the other person feel understood, validated, and cared for. You'll both like each other better.

Discussion

Wayne: I'm curious whether your approach applies to both genders. For example, you said in chapter 2 that men didn't benefit as much from gratitude.

Sherri: My article addresses the marriage relationship, and looks at the value of positive emotions that make us willing to be vulnerable to another person. From this vulnerability can come love and joy. So yes, my advice applies to both genders, and as with all happiness suggestions, "fit" is important. Are you married? Just wondering...

Wayne: I have been happily married for 20 years – and we are still very much in love. Our friends often comment on how good our marriage is.

I had a discussion with my partner about your article, and we agreed with most (not all) of what you said.

We would add mutual respect for our differences, talking to each other, and understanding that bad stuff happens.

I've also observed a difference between men and women with respect to gratitude, so I avoid talking about gratitude with male clients unless it's a high value. As you say – one size does not fit all, and the same applies to gratitude.

By the way the irony is that I have higher levels of gratitude than my partner.

Sherri: Congratulations on your long-lived marriage. I've been married 25 years. The friendship and flexibility you mention are certainly important in any relationship. I did not make an exhaustive list of things that work. For instance, I meditate nearly every day, and I find mindfulness is a great tool for dealing with the unexpected in life.

Steve: Great article. I believe that mature and successful relationships are rooted in love that is unconditional, altruistic, and full of gratitude and appreciation. It is within upon this overarching type of love that Eros can exist.

NOTES

These chapters are all based on articles published online in Positive Psychology News Daily. They have been edited to remove jargon and research details that readers might find distracting. However, for those who want to know the research that supports the statements and suggestions, there is a link below to a page on the Web that has links to all the original unabridged articles. We did not try to reproduce that research information in these notes because it is openly accessible online to anyone who is curious enough to look for it.

Please feel free to post comments or questions there. Authors and other members of the positive psychology community continue to respond to comments for all articles, new and old.

http://positivepsychologynews.com/books/gratitude

The notes included here serve two purposes. First they describe concepts, such as character strengths and the power of positive emotions that are used in practically every chapter because they are so fundamental to positive psychology. For authors, these are the ABCs of the subject, so we often take for granted that readers will know them. Second we acknowledge the scholars whose work underlies and supports the points we make in this book. Many of them have written books that are very practical and useful resources if you want to explore these topics further.

Most chapters in this book owe a debt to Robert Emmons, a pre-eminent scholar of gratitude, who wrote the book, *Thanks: How the New Science of Gratitude Can Make You Happier*. The sixth chapter, Gratitude in Trying Times, seems particularly appropriate for the worries of today.

Character strengths also appear in many chapters. What are your own particular character strengths? One way to find out is to take the online instrument called the Values-in-Action (VIA) signature strength test at http://viasurvey.org (free, with fee for more detailed report). The VIA is a scientifically validated tool for measuring character strengths. The 240 questions elicit your unique constellation of strengths and identify your signature strengths, that is, the ones you most frequently express.

The theme of positive emotion appears in practically every chapter in this book. According to psychologist Barbara Fredrickson at the University of North Carolina, positive emotions broaden our thoughts and behaviors, as well as build important durable resources, including social connectedness and physical health. Her book, *Positivity*, is another great source for practical suggestions.

Psychologist Sonja Lyubomirsky outlines some compelling research on the restorative power of gratitude in her book, *The How of Happiness*. Expressing gratitude is the first happiness activity in her list of twelve. She describes several specific activities that help us build the benefits of gratitude into our lives.

Further Reading

Emmons, R. (2007). *Thanks! How the new science of grati-tude can make you happier.* Boston: Houghton-Mifflin. Books.

Ben-Shahar, T. (2007). *Happier: Learn the Secrets to Daily Joy and Lasting Fulfillment.* McGraw-Hill Professional. De-scribes the gratitude journal and gratitude letters exercises.

Emmons, R. (2003). Acts of gratitude in organizations. In K. S. Cameron, J. E. Dutton, & R. E. Quinn (Eds.), *Positive Or-ganizational Scholarship: Foundations of a New Discipline.* (pp. 81-93). San Francisco: Berrett-Kohler.

Fredrickson, B. L. (2009). *Positivity: Groundbreaking Re-search Reveals How to Embrace the Hidden Strength of Posi-tive Emotions, Overcome Negativity, and Thrive.* New York: Crown.

Grenville-Cleave, B., Boniwell, I., & Tessina, T. (2009). *The Happiness Equation: 100 Factors That Can Add To or Sub-tract From Your Happiness.* Adams Media.

Lyubomirsky, S. (2008). *The How of Happiness: A Scientific Approach to Getting the Life You Want.* New York: Penguin Press.

Miller, C. A. & Frisch, M. B. (2009). *Creating Your Best Life: The Ultimate Life List Guide.* New York: Sterling. The book includes a form for the Three Blessings exercise.

Peterson, C. (2006). *A Primer in Positive Psychology.* New York: Oxford University Press.

Reis, H.T., Gable, S. L. (2003). Toward a Positive Psychology of Relationships. In C. L. Keyes & J. Haidt (Eds.), *Flourishing: Positive Psychology and the Life Well-Lived*, 129-159. Washington, D.C.: American Psychological Association. This paper explores the active constructive responding approach described at the beginning of chapter 19.

Richard, M. (2006). *Happiness: A Guide to Developing Life's Most Important Skill.* London: Atlantic Books.

Seligman, M.E.P., (2002). *Authentic Happiness.* New York: Free Press.

Thatchenkery, T. & Metzker, C. (2006). *Appreciative Intelligence: Seeing the Mighty Oak in the Acorn.* San Francisco: Berrett-Koehler.

Vaillant, G. (1998). *Aging Well: Surprising Guideposts to a Happier Life from the Landmark Harvard Study of Adult Development.* New York: Little Brown.

Vaillant, G. (1998). *Adaptations to Life.* New York: Harvard University Press.

Vaillant, G. (2008). *Spiritual Evolution: A Scientific Defense of Faith.* Broadway Books.

Illustrator

 **Kevin Gillespie** is a designer and illustrator. He has been working in the footwear design world for the last fifteen years. These days he is providing illustrations and graphic design services for a wide variety of purposes.

You can see many examples of his work on his website: http://kevingillespie.com.